View from the North Ten

Poems after Mark Rothko's *No. 15*

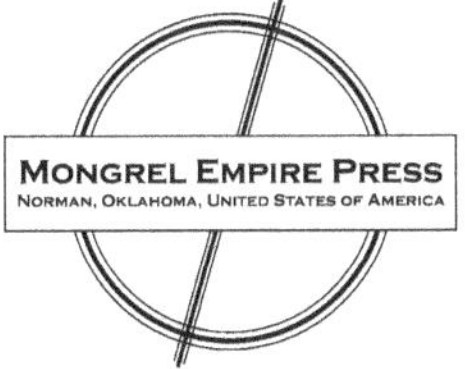

Norman, Oklahoma
2013

FIRST EDITION, 2013

View from the North Ten: Poems after Mark Rothko's No. 15

ISBN 978-0-9851337-3-3

Cover Image:
The North Ten © Jenni Wichern 2013

MONGREL EMPIRE PRESS
NORMAN, OK

ONLINE CATALOGUE: WWW.MONGRELEMPIRE.ORG

This publisher is a proud member of

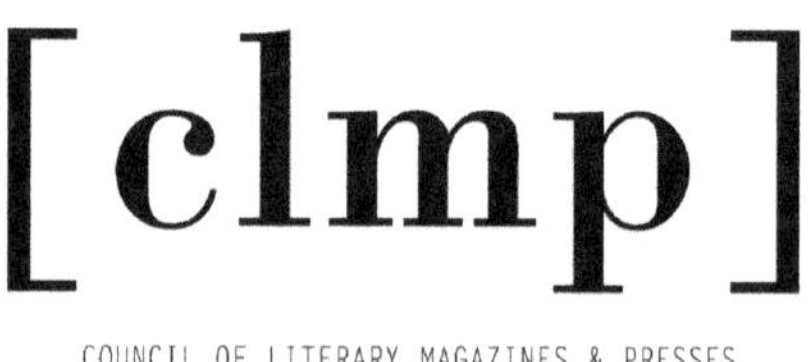

COUNCIL OF LITERARY MAGAZINES & PRESSES
www.clmp.org

Book Design: Mongrel Empire Press using iWork Pages

View from the North Ten

Poems after Mark Rothko's *No. 15*

Dave Malone

Acknowledgments

I would like to thank my partner Jenni Wichern for the gorgeous cover picture and the author photo. A heartfelt thank you goes to publisher, Jeanetta Calhoun Mish, who believed in this book and created its lovely design.

Thanks also to two dear friends and colleagues, Darrelyn Saloom and Matt Brennan, for their suggestions on improving this manuscript. And thank you to Teri Moore, who gave me a genuine introduction to Rothko.

Some of these poems, often in earlier versions, were first published elsewhere. Grateful acknowledgement to the editors of these journals and magazines:

@Urban: "Picking Blackberries"

The Cape Rock: "Hog Red"

Cave Region Review: "Ten-Pointer" and "Tongue of the Osage"

CircleShow: "White"

Crosstimbers: "Solitude" as "Golden Coats"

Elder Mountain: A Journal of Ozark Studies: "Fault" as "Red Dust" and "Blackberry Cobbler" as "White" in volume 2 (2010) and "Union" in volume 3 (2011).

Fogged Clarity: "Ceiling Corners of the Existential"

Kansas City Voices: "Red" as "Anthony's Red"

Kansas English: "Rothko's Red on Yellow," and "Grilled Cheese and Ketchup"

Kentucky English Bulletin: "Cradle" and "No One Could Accuse" as "Curve Ball: A Love Poem"

The Meadow: "Nature's Gold"

San Pedro River Review: "View from the North Ten"

Stone's Throw: "Red Center"

Visions (Northwest Arkansas Community College): "Witching Hour"

Willows Wept Review: "Almost Confident" (Winter 2010) and "Tornado Yellow" as "Snake Charmer" (Summer 2011)

"Rothko's Reds" originally appeared as part of a guest post, "Coming Home to Red," on the Tweetspeak Poetry blog.

"Blackberry Cobbler" will also appear in *Yonder Mountain: An Ozarks Anthology* from the University of Arkansas Press, 2013.

Contents

Part I

Part II

Part III

A picture lives by companionship, expanding and quickening in the eyes of the sensitive observer.

—Mark Rothko

Part I

1 | Red Center

Could Rothko have known
you are so much woman
when oil sprung from inside, not daubs,
but red and yellow gashes
slicing from his arms. A tall man
invisible in front of canvas nearly twice his size.

Supernova bursts spread top and bottom,
logged in redshift of his making.
No above and below in three-dimension space.
Only star fuel where you and I take shape,
apparitions partitioned here only for explanation.

That midsection is curious.
A cloaked croak for critics.
But intersection for you and me.
A pair of nebula
firing through atmosphere,
nothing but light and heat,
like these August afternoons
west of the Delta where farm fields,
stripped of beans and cotton,
reach for the horizon, a magenta strip
of oil paint, vanishing into black.

2 | High Note

I bled out from the mouth that afternoon
you trundled off with the conductor.
Two weeks later, I stole his baton
from shadow and proceeded to direct
evening traffic at the foothill of the Square.
A mere high note away from your apartment,
actors and addicts, drag queens
and working mothers
joined hands in the street
to put Ravel into traffic
and turn your heart toward me.

3 | White Blouse

The afternoon you wore white,
herons slunk away from the banks of the Eleven Point,
kids on Aid Avenue abandoned chalky chalk,
and the white collars at the bank
traded in for blue chambray and bib overalls.

A simple thing.
A white blouse.
A button undone.
An old standard
that Tony Bennett could harp
in his sleep.
The fine sidewalk crack
that makes an S
in front of your porch.

4 | Tornado Yellow

Sky hums tornado yellow.
Your sundress ruby
as hog-plump tomatoes
we saw twelve storm miles back
at Dexter. The Hispanic mama
couldn't put down *Grapes of Wrath* babies,
so you tucked triplets of what was due her—
bills beneath ripe watermelons bulging.

The truck drops into farm valley.
My eyes lock on your outstretched finger
to the old homestead, barely larger
than a jigsaw puzzle piece on the window.
A silver silo bleats into the wind,
and dark cumulus clouds wag stooping shoulders
like schoolteachers bent after seasons awry.

Many years ago, all the sons of your stepfather
disappeared for the city and left your tom-girl nature
to scythe weeds so corn could mature
into milky adulthood. When the stalks pushed past
your stepdad's whiskey-thin frame,
he shouted down like an impotent Moses,
rock hard on conquering his people.

You rocketed on the anniversary
of the moon landing, rangy tassels on the corn
burning russet in July clouds until the sky
tore apart like today. A yellow hum
burning through a crimson dress.

5 | Bent on Floating

You have nearly
forgotten the past
when your laugh
fanned sunflowers
back into black eyes,
crisp as wolves'
in the brambled brush.

Beside the peeling farmhouse,
you held on that hill all afternoon
while your ex anointed with piss
that marriage, now only his.
Your back, like summer's canoe,
land-locked and berthed,
sunk into Illinois farm dirt and arrowhead
as light climbed over your knees at noon.
By five, he leaned against the clapboard
where he puked pilsner. October slid
maroon bottle caps onto the curvy
elms above your hips arched upward
like stern hulls shimmed,
bent on floating.

6 | Blood Red

Menstrual blood on gold sheets
is stamped by your knuckle,
then fingers flower open
to pull me into silk flesh
warmer than these sheets.

We curl up into red
until your blood is a shawl,
an afghan, a toothbrush, and a razor.
We need not leave the bed
for the fool's gold horizon
or the sneak attack September sun
riding eastern blond beach clouds and shrinking
the days into autumn numbers.

When your period is over,
a crimson rain cloud rips the rafters
of the house until our bodies split
underneath oak beams, two cherry blossoms
floating from ceiling to floor,
their scent slipping away in the night air.

7 | White

Before one dives into the painting,
all gleams white. Then Rothko emerges
river-red, gold-boned. The viewer
should start on the cliff edges. Alone.
A bashful swimmer about to be dunked.

8 | Grain Blond

I hail from a line
of alcoholics
as long
as Missouri Delta
train tracks
yawning from one
grain blond horizon
to the next.

You sparred
all my forefathers
possum-trapped
in the spiny teeth
of your old man.

On a porch
as short
as a sawed-off
twelve-gauge,
we hold hands and marvel
at the height
of the sycamore tree
leaning far to the left.

9 | Tongue of the Osage

The Missouri River separates us.
This russet summer snake slinking
sideways across grape and groused hills.
Stone arrowheads slice the mud
after a downpour, and even the river
turns the color of copperheads,
matching the curls of my hair
as wild as buffalo to the Osage
whose flint ignites dirt dusk.

The great river eats the weak.
We have to cross
for you to kiss my eyelids
and for me to spoon you at night.
That birch bark canoe I crafted
one summer to get back to my roots
only made me hate both blood lines
squawking through me, jagged as ripped meat
dangling from crow beaks.
But by God or the Great Spirit,
the damn thing held water.

On rose-fire mornings,
the auburn craft can be seen
waltzing on the water,
one fierce wind away from docking.
Sometimes, a man and woman
embrace in sycamore shadow.
Sometimes, one rows alone
with a breeze of syllables,
hushed low,
the names of flint, fire,
river, and union
in the tongue of the Osage.

10 | No One Could Accuse

Lollipop-red stitches
of the baseball whiz
by my throat
as if I'd laid it out there
like a chicken resigned
to the afterlife.

Pops McGee doesn't have
to waddle down
from the American Legion field
to drip tobacco juice on my cleats
and bark a reminder you have
a good curve ball.

You'll pitch until there's
no arm left and make yourself
an ice prosthetic that evening.
It's then at midnight
when the painkillers,
smelling of too ripe beeswax,
have died a simple scratch
in the box score,
I find you barefoot,
sunburned, slinging back
milk out of the jug,
where no one could accuse you
of throwing like a girl.

11 | Blood Makes It So

I know your past.
A katydid song never sleeping.
The demands you had to shoulder
while your ex rubbed his legs,
a croaking chorus.

Your new farm paints the bluff
better than light from Orion.
You take on alone
because blood makes it so.

I love the Jupiter red
of your lips and the scratching rhythm
of jazz on your drawing table.

I am in the dizzy haze of the Milky Way
where I eat dust to forge poems
with nebula fire for backbones.

A tarp of stars haunts the night.
Gold and red fire. Only visible
together.

12 | Nature's Gold

Smoke polkas above the pines
the night I burn my novel.
In fire, you bake your old man's heart,
a blackened raisin. I bury a brother.
You raise a daughter from the dead.

Our losses spread out nature's gold
as bountiful as needles beneath
Scotch pines lining our drive.
What we can't say
chisels ginger cracks
into the harvest moon.

13 | December Stars

My body shines numb red
like those sandwich bags of blood
refrigerated behind hospital glass.
I sprawl on my back at Ozark pond.
Bullfrogs croak as deep as Italian tenors
and the earthy smell of horseshit
looms softer than cattails.

Blue blood floats in my hands.
My fingers lost to me, the only
geography that registers
is the hip curve my skin remembers.
The peach sun skips across my toes
and changes the pond.

I won't move for hours
even after December stars
smolder. Comfort may come
inside night's shawl
where your body once
posted a fixed orbit.

14 | Ceiling Corners of the Existential

I wake up in my bedroom not knowing.
It's unclear if you're star-gazing
outside the tent in that shitty park
in Tonganoxie, Kansas. Or if you're naked,
fridge-side rummaging for milk
and any sliver of chocolate kindness.

I get lost while tracing
the topography of the white ceiling.
Tiny roads, mountains rise.
I can't tell if I'm above all of it, gazing down,
or if I'm beneath it somehow,
hugging inside the earth's endoderm
where I suffocate above core and mantle,
eager to surface like bluebirds I saw hatch once.
Milky bodies, blind, dumb birds.

I don't hear you.
Absence of kitchen door percussion
that cuts out sleep. And I don't feel you outside,
your pose tilted as if you could catch Orion
raining on your forehead.
Only this white haze of mountain
and country road that fades out
as it reaches the corners.

15 | Cradle

The two bourbon-colored barns
hold watch over the back five acres.
Two pairs of overalls stained maroon
as if dark Ozark clay climbed up the sides.

A May thunderboomer knocked out
all the barn glass like teeth. The storm
punished acorns into the ground,
and a post oak rooted between the barns.

Summer days, the sun writes red
into the clay, until inky thumbprints
crack down the drive.
The oak and the barns
now bend at the arms, and dusk
light is cradled there—pink skin against
leaf and fading wood.

Part II

1 | Injustice

The tornado taller than the courthouse
shredded the Miller farmstead
as quick and easy as the deputy
piggy-thumbing and plopping parking tickets.
At Brenda's Café, some want
to talk about injustice.
But the locals say there's water
under that farm. A lightning rod
for bad weather—yellow sky and wind
drawing venom out of the ground.

2 | Gold Light

Gold light wiggles out
from a space in the red brick.
Winter winds haunt this former church
you live in with your three babies.
Huddled in a bathtub, you push down
infant heads until they disappear inside
homemade quilts. Beside broken pews,
woodstove piping glows like a forest fire.

3 | Auburn Beard

My auburn beard fuzz
rests against your shoulder,
its summer tan just now beginning.
You swear the garden
will make this year.
The slow light of morning
crests the bedroom window sill.
On hardwood floor,
sunlight and shadow collide.

4 | Primary Colors

Why jab more gold at the bottom?
As if to say humans must have a basis
for blooming in this blood-boiling body.
And the slashes of coffee. Do we need
a river-brown religion to save us from damnation?
And the red middle finger. Do you antagonize
a plump politic where brick crushes brick?
And the square canvas. Do you hold life still
as a color wheel when nothing holds still?

5 | Red Plaid

You're a shadow in the north ten
where you fix fence with baling wire
and patience. You don't wear
my red plaid or my Levi's
like last night against the blood fire,
and the ghost appears again.
I know what you're afraid of.
It lurks in a black bottle in a shed
in central Illinois, where your ex beat
his throat into it, like a fireman
slugging a blaze he can't quell.
And you fear being consumed.
You don't know I understand,
once drizzled over camp flame
in the Manzano Mountains
towering above Albuquerque.

6 | Copper Sky, Red Suns

My vision gets lost
inside the raku-fired cups
our friend built, one for each
of us. Your vessel darker,
with brooding mountains, a copper sky,
and a pair of red suns. I do not know
where you've placed your gift—whether
in the barn studio, on the porch drawing table,
perhaps inside your rib cage
to pound out sun-beats of loneliness.

7 | Red

You pull away from me as if red can lose red.
We boiled over one night. The moon turned ruby,
the trunk of the oak churned a crimson volcano,
the Missouri River, a bleeding artery.
I won't dam this up. I won't pull back—
how the night draws its knees
up into the sky and lets dusk red pour through.

8 | Witching Hour

The armadillo husk glows gold
on Ozark blacktop. Surely, the creature
left Arkansas and roadside tarantulas
for a haven of ripe insects
singing love choruses
against verdant swamp,
almost Texas neon in the silver dusk
before Ozark sun whimpers
into Kansas.

I've tilled the north ten so far down
the devil pops the ceiling with his pitchfork
though he knows full well
witch's dance is two full moons out.
I have nothing left,
save a few arms and legs
and three cans of beer inside.
I could crawl into that armadillo shell
and hide out in the blanched remainder
of what once was. But this red,
beating heart drowns out witches' noise
and the siren call of sleep
of the overturned earth.

9 | Solitude

You were hell-bent
on saving those golden-coated calves
as if your small hand
could flex fat enough to stave off
the circle of slim coyotes
that pushed through the drought
and cornered those babies.

Your grandfather's bullwhip
of the self-same cowhide
transformed you into a whirling dervish,
praising some god coyotes don't know.
With a ripped leg, you mounted the porch,
and I drove us two hours to the city for care.
It was the last I'd see of you for weeks.
The calves survived and ate clover
until their coats gleamed burgundy like blood.

10 | Surprise Lilies

The softest girl
in boy's Levi's
is almost
eight and a half.
She has abandoned
her bike in front of corn
three times her size and swaying
in July heat.

She eyes me, buried
face-deep in the third rangy row,
corn-scratched face as if I shaved
blind. My brown eyes, raccoon-swollen,
after you gave your word
you'd closed your heart
like the surprise lilies on the lane.
The child sees the thistle bayonet
burst through my back, and she
chugs, knees-up to her waist,
the top of her head
disappearing below the flat edge
of the summer-brown lane.

11 | Ten-Pointer

You might as well have gutted me
like the buck you took that first winter.
The ten-pointer's entrails
spilled on the barn floor
like so much rotten ketchup.
Your mouth kept knotted
like the makeshift fix
to the gambrel. And you stood over
the mess of his life
until I toed it back into the earth.

12 | Fault

I wouldn't mind the time apart—
the Tectonic Plates beneath the Gulf
riding herd close to the ones
below Ozark hills, but I know
how mountain dolomite feels in the hand,
how gravel-road-red dust hovers in August air.
You ain't coming back in September.
The Black Angus in the flat
fall in the heat like fainting goats,
wary of a milk moon predator.
The New Madrid fault tears
wide like your Ford pickup
barreling across the thin bridge
into Cairo, Illinois. You'll cross
just before the dry earth splits
and the fault caves in.

13 | Crows

I know it's the end
when I cut myself shaving,
and blood pools at my feet
larger than concentric circles
at crime scenes on Hollywood TV.
I wipe off the white porcelain,
so the blood can join itself
and mix up like a martini
shaken, stirred, and gulped.
The wood floorboards creak
under the weight of the Missouri.
The river of blood leaves me chinless
and sweating in my blue jeans
as I hear the porch door swing out.
Rusted springs squawk like crows
at last night's windows. Lean, famished birds
spy a woman in the dark
with some stranger rocking in her bed.

14 | Walnut Fruit

A Hollywood heart
weighs less than a real heart,
ingests fewer calories,
and is about as broad
as a frog's hind legs.
You'd have thought
I'd browsed that movie script
once or twice on the farm.
Lazy afternoons when the baler
gets jammed and Three Finger Collins
stares the machine down
into Sunday solemnity.
You knew enough of Gwyneth Paltrow charm
to write yourself in.
A white dress, the magic hour
when dusk fans out crimson
and purple like exotic flora.
You turning away from my legs
straddling the rattle-trap tractor.
My heart cracked open
as messy as walnut fruit.

15 | Grilled Cheese and Ketchup

One might say Rothko painted
a grilled-cheese sandwich with ketchup,
paving way for Warhol antics
and creamy tomato soup,
but Rothko would rebuke such silliness
though I'm always tempted
to eat up his canvases
with a glass of milk.

And he might have gone for that,
knowing immersion in milk
and grilled-cheese is a decent fate.
He might even clink a silo-tall glass with me
when I showed him how the universes within
expand this way and that,
no true lines in his painting.

Part III

1 | Scenes in No. 15

You are the whole painting.

The entire farm on the bluff
above the Missouri. The gravel drive
with silver scat-chat slinking down the hill
like jazz dripping beer-keg sweat
into pools glowing in electric blue light.

The gold teeth of the blues man
who stomps boots at the shanty
marked with a homemade sign
before you and I ballooned into this world.

The once red-haired beauty
with a matching taffeta dress who crunches
like popcorn as she shimmies from faux-wood bar
to a stage barely larger than her pumps
glowing pumpkin orange.

The whizzing ceiling fan in the middle
with the brown whir of stolen hooch below
as it chugs down the river bluff
glugging like the Missouri River itself
when she slams shots against the shore.

2 | Giving Way to Autumn

When we made love,
time disappeared into a knapsack
you lugged over the Big Piney River
and made a pillow of later
when coyotes crafted the dark
into shrill C notes desperate
to dart below the treble clef.

On blond pine needles
our backs, arched like logs,
host a cosmos of beetles,
brittle wood, and moss warm
between our legs.

3 | View from the North Ten

Rocky moon rips
through icy November sky.
Alone on the farm, I walk
the north ten in my ropers and pull plaid
to cover the blade-ready throat.
Separation feels so absolute
it takes on the ugliness of divorce:
house axed in half, a child's bee bonnet
sliced like bread, the unkempt lawn
filled with cavities where love lost.

This feeling is mostly myth. Or is it?
When you're gone, you're gone.
No legalese nor poetry speak—
compass this, compass that—
will change your course of NNE.
I travel our favorite part of the farm
because when you're here, you're here.

4 | Picking Blackberries

It's not a pretty dance.
Unlike the USO flavor of the 40s
where GIs with buzz cuts
and Bogey half-smiles
wooed ladies with Coke bottle
shaped dresses, accentuating every turn.

Some of the best blackberries
like to rest, throned like kings,
bulging paunches, with thorny
footmen at their sides. A few sword thrusts
and your fingers are pink, shades lighter
than the juice you seek.

But you've come for the adventure of it.
To push back the prickly advances
of smaller suitors, to sidestep poison ivy's
greenest touch. You go into the deep
where little light passes, you're off balance
and leaning. But this is where the truth is—
the culmination of earth years and finding
the sweetness in your lover's brambly hair,
the ripping touch, the poisonous days
you survive, to break through into the deep,
where the sweetest fruit grows.

5 | Hog Red

You said you'd butcher
the hog if I didn't.
A chef from St. Louis
taught you how to shoot
zombie-eyed and determined.
Over dirt coffee, we rest
while the windows jiggle
over the sink like the jowls
of Sharpy—I'd affectionately
called our gift from Pops McGee
for baling his south forty.

You crave cream. I smell the buttercup
tongue sweetness on you now
while I ponder the fuzzy muzzle
of Sharpy, inches below the spot
I'm going to extinguish his wiggly
momentum carrying him through life.
In the barn, the knives lurk
Hollywood-slasher sharp,
and the silver gambrel hangs high,
a gallows for tallow-taking above sleeping fur.
My .22 and knife on the porch begin
to squawk like restless chickens.

You pour our last morning cup.
Your eyes once green now blue
with December ice. I will get up soon
because only hog and wood will get us
through winter. Outside, wind hooks
the windows into clattering cymbals,

just before a pistol shot pops
into a squeal, and a knife lands
a jugular cut, blood warming
clay ground and blond hay.

6 | Rothko's Reds

We are joined at the hip bones
like Rothko's reds. Slight spaces
between, like woman-man skin
sticking, unsticking—blotchy fuzz
Rothko wrists into the painting.
No matter how you triangulate the canvas,
you see us. Naked pulsing red mists—
no boundaries on land,
pond, and autumn gold field.

7 | Surviving Lost

We get misplaced on John Brown's Highway
in eastern dusk-red Kansas until the two-laner,
as wide as Laverne's pink hips
at the Nowhere Diner we just passed,
turns into one line of gravel the size of crows
haunting the rusty barb wire to the south.
Your lexicon lost lost
one year on the farm
when you learned its blueprint
in sneakered footprints as you hid out
from your older brothers
with hay-bale-tossed shoulders.

You wouldn't know lost
again for twenty years—the afternoon
your ex rammed the pickup
into the silo and splattered corn
over the windshield like sleet.
One of your daughters held out
a lollipop-red fist to you,
the other a yellow, broken kneecap.

8 | Rothko's Red on Yellow

There's a look it carries.
A feeling a librarian must have
when she begins to fall in love
with the idea of rows and rows
of books.

And the sounds—doors engineered
not to slam, people's mouths shaped like Os
with barometers on them, where pressure
maxes out at a key level. And the distance in the aisles,
the decisions made on which magazines
and newspapers shall color
the shelves like newlywed fiestaware.

9 | Blackberry Cobbler

The night you wore your white blouse into the barn
where cloggers yanked up dust to their knees,
all the corn farmers pulled at pressed shirts
behind bib overalls in order to breathe,
overcome by a similar feeling they knew
in their muscled backs when pressed against
church pews their granddaddies made
before the only real war.

Pies perched on shiny red-checkered tables
and stretched out like barb wire
plucky with red blackberries
that had been set on waiting for June heat
before turning belly up.
On the far end, by that woman horse Delilah,
you plopped the blackberry cobbler
your Granny Rowlett showed you how to make
the summer you visited the Ozarks,
the one afternoon she kept you out of the canoe
and hot box with the boys from the crossroads.

It's this blackberry dance, the high red note,
the gold crust, all against your white blouse
and tan hands—this is the refrain
that stopped the cloggers
and silenced their jingle taps
and turned the square-dancers
into elliptical waltzers. It's this music
that cost me two Andrew Jacksons
as I held the bills high in the barn
over the sad hound-dog eyes
of Shooter McKenzie who hoped
he had a dating chance.

10 | Union

Against honey sheets
with back-loving softness
of thread counts to die for,
we plunge into a gold
and shimmery death
like going down for Christ
in Ozark river waters—the preacher's
white linen and galoshes sparkle
in our new life while mourning doves
coo gray softness in sycamore limbs
as we commit the greatest union
of God and man. Broken bones join.
Hips meet as black snakes slither
end to end. Distant tan knobs
dissolve into plateau, and storm clouds
burst magnolia skin to life.

11 | The Axis of Mars

A windstorm on Mars
sets you off. Your golden skin
from cycling through Colorado
simmers into lava rock,
and your hips glow crimson fuzz
blowing magenta dust
in swan circles around my thighs.

Your hips gleam cycle hard
as you turn the painting sideways
and shift your sunburned thighs
to dig in for me, the axis
of Mars pulling through you,
a ray of red light, dancing on
the planet's horizon, your legs wrapped
into my oxblood paint fire and around
your own gold blonde insides.

12 | The Real Slough

The mud-red-caked gar chugs close
enough to your feet for you to feel
the likelihood of a catfish
you know how to nail up
and skin with pliers as quick
as Granny Rowlett could pull through
a stitch row in forthcoming winter quilts
for eight grandkids.

The June day is itself soaked
in blue-beaded sweat like the ripped chambray
on your older brother's back. He crouches
six waddling paces behind you. After enough rain
to mud the well water for days, the slough
stretches from the Illinois River
into the corn crop cowering in encroaching
waters hip high.

In gold-flecked mire, your arms
reach between your muck boots
to push the shadowy fish to the mud below
where you grip the straggler into brief submission.
You yank the beast from the backwater
into blue Midwest sunlight to find
not a whiskery catfish but the silver
hypodermic needles of gar teeth.
So quick almost one motion of ripping
from river into the air,
you launch the spiky-mouthed gar
over your shoulders into space,
to ricochet off your brother's hip waders.
But you wouldn't know until years later
when you abandoned the farm
where the real slough lay.

13 | Divorce

Black Angus bay
with elephant bravado
beneath post oaks—Towers of Babel
to Delta gods on Jack Flat.
You've heard that tree-topping holler
in the hollow at the old farmstead
where dumb, slit-eyed steers
trampled brush for digging contests
that didn't count.

Jamming the Nova into fourth,
you're about to rise above the valley,
but bull bellows awaken your baby girls.
With the woods as dark and deep
as Tolkien stories, you sing the only hymns
you remember to these daughters
as slight and narrow as Arkansas blacktop.

14 | Space

I give you enough space to love me.
The red barn, the south forty, the railroad,
the Ozark knob past Poe Hill,
the Delta, and the Mississippi.
You grip my back
when we make love
until the foundation
of southern Missouri
quakes above the New Madrid.
Your lips tight, wet,
open full like a harvest moon
sneaking up the horizon
over the mansard roof of the barn.

15 | Almost Confident

I never knew white lingered
in the gold. Like that time I made off
for Chicago while you dumped cattle
into the south ten. I broke down
somewhere past Wrigley in a snowstorm
that dusted our Black Angus but stranded me
in the Chevy for days. Opening truck doors
sprayed snow into my hair like the time
we woke at dawn the first week on the farm,
and flakes slid off the roof and lanced our eyes.
When Rothko painted fifteen,
he snaked our love story inside his wrists
only to let go like so much breath
launched on Ozark winter mornings—
the steam rises as wispy wood smoke,
almost confident it's alive.

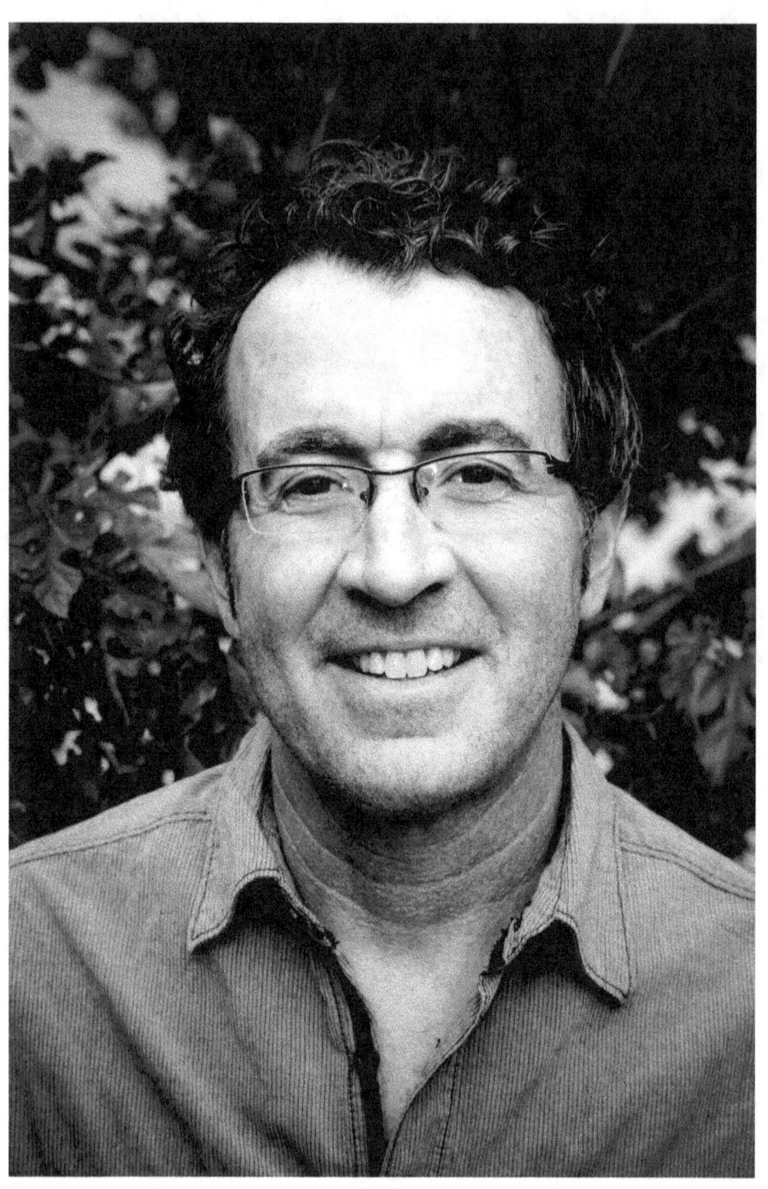

The Author

Dave Malone was born in Rolla, Missouri, and grew up in both Missouri and Kansas. He attended Ottawa University and received a master's degree in English from Indiana State University.

He is the author of four previous collections: *Seasons in Love, Under the Sycamore, 23 Sonnets*, and *Poems to Love and the Body.*

His poems have also appeared in many online and print literary journals including *The Cape Rock, Cave Region Review, Crosstimbers, Elder Mountain: A Journal of Ozark Studies, Kentucky English Bulletin, Mid Rivers Review,* and *San Pedro River Review.*

In April of 2011, one of his Twitter poems aired on the "Muses and Metaphor" series from NPR's *Tell Me More* radio program. He publishes a monthly e-newsletter, *If I Had a Nickel,* whose title derives from the sentiment of his rascally grandfather.

In addition to his involvement in several small business ventures, Dave teaches film courses at Missouri State University-West Plains. Dave lives with his partner Jenni Wichern and their child Caiden in the Missouri Ozarks, where his family roots go back prior to the Civil War.

Dave's interests, bordering on obsessions, include Alan Watts, Ozark culture, and minor league baseball. To connect with Dave, visit *davemalone.net* or *twitter.com/dzmalone*.

www.ingramcontent.com/pod-product-compliance
Lightning Source LLC
LaVergne TN
LVHW010841120826
845149LV00020B/3440